LIVING
IN THE
Spirit
of
God

LIVING IN THE Spirit of God

LARNA WOODS

LitPrime
"Your story is our priority"

LitPrime Solutions
East Brunswick Office Evolution
1 Tower Center Boulevard, Ste 1510
East Brunswick, NJ 08816
www.litprime.com
Phone: 1-800-981-9893

Published by LitPrime Solutions: 11/13/2024

ISBN: 979-8-88703-434-8(sc)
ISBN: 979-8-88703-435-5(e)

Library of Congress Control Number: 2024920661

Contents

Introduction ix

Chapter 1. "Struggle between Good and Evil" . . . 1
Chapter 2. "Oh my God what a ride" 8
Chapter 3. "Spirit Lifted Me" 12
Chapter 4. "You know not How I Come" 18
Chapter 5. "Let the Story be Told, the
            Challenger" 21
Chapter 6. "The Stranger in my Life" 25
Chapter 7. "Spiritual Visitor During The Night" 32
Chapter 8. "Grandma Mary's Visit" 35
Chapter 9. "Out of The Mouths of Babs" 38
Chapter 10. "Inception, the Story of Myra" 43
Chapter 11. "Million Doller Plot Spoiled" 50
Chapter 12. "A Night to Remember With
            Rev. Dye" 58
Chapter 13. "Spirituals Healing Power" 64
Chapter 14. "God gave me a Way Out" 72
Chapter 15. "Lena Amonte, Spiritualist" 77

Conclusion 85

"Dedicated to the Believers of the Holy Spirit of God"

I'm dedicating this book, the second edition of "Living in The Spirit of God" to the many Spiritualists and friends that have encountered the spiritual entities of our universe, with the hope and knowledge of the spiritualist involvement of what we call Spiritualism, we will learn to live with the knowledge that this rim of our life is real and it's a fact to be acknowledged, for our lifetime and for the future. Those that will become aware of what God has for us and become a part of His miracles and experiences, wonders, and activities, will take this knowledge for what it really is and refer to it as spiritual gifts of the Holy Spirit of God. God has given to us the help and guidance and in many cases protection for us in this universe of ours.

Introduction

The second edition of this book, Living in The Spirit of God, is a number of short true stories, about my life at various stages. It is the experiences and the devastation in certain situations that occurred in my life as I went through life's different avenues. Being guided by help from my God and His Angels, I knew along the way that helped would come along this difficult path. In the past and now I had help in overcoming obstacles that were placed in my path which helped me in life to emerge as a confident and self-sufficient person.

I knew that along the way that help would come from the Holy Spirit, helping me in my difficult times. In the past and now I knew that I would eventually overcome the devastation that was placed before me.

Sometimes I would feel like I could give up, but because of my faith I kept believing and pushing on. This came about because of the many experiences that I had had dealing with the spiritual world and its entities. And for all of this I give thanks to my God and His Spiritual Angels.

Chapter 1

"Struggle between Good and Evil"

It's been several years since I've written and I hope to put together a second edition and continuation of the first "Living in the Spirit of God" book. This chapter is an account of the all enduring battle with the spirit of God and that of the opposing demonic forces of evil that are in the world today.

I was a young woman in my early twenties and single. Living on my own with a year old son and barely making it day by day in a small city in Western Michigan. Being filled with remorse because of many factors about my son and being a single mother life was not easy at all. Things had become very difficult to manage at that stage, having fallen in love by looking for love for all the wrong reasons and in all the wrong places. It appeared to me that I had made so many mistakes and so many wrong decisions at that time in my life. I sensed a great deal of regret come over me like a flood so many times leaving me very despondent and wondering what if anything I would end up doing next. The only thing I felt I had to live for was my son which I love so very much. I was very thankful to God for giving me the love of a child this I believe this was God giving me unconditional love that I had always wished for and hope for most of my life. This stemming from the type of life I had grown up with in my mother's and father's home. It was very abusive my father was shell shocked. I constantly prayed that things for myself and my son had happened under better and different circumstances. These incidences just seem to come back to haunt me continuously. Thoughts that wouldn't stop even though I pray constantly the pain was so great and it stayed.

There were dark times also. I had no job needed to finish school. I had suffered through another beating when I left my mother's and father's home; I had one more subject to finish before graduation. That's when I left to stay with a beautician that my mother knew for years. I finish school and took some additional classes at the skill center. I constantly continue to think that there has to be more to life than this kind of life. I had never heard the words I love you or you did a good job from my parents. Or even thank you for something I had done for my mother or father as I was growing up. Warmth and compassion never happens in the home as far as I could remember. This I long for as a child and even as an adult, because of this I made an oath to God and to my son that I would be different and I would do and show by hugging and saying words of love and compassion to my children as they grow up, even as they would become adults. I believe that these words of affection and expression are basics for the needs for all humans for survival. With all this in my life I begin to question my life more and the intentions that God had for me. It became more intensified as time went by. More and more I had feelings of there being an entity or entities in my surroundings and in my home in my presence. It was very discerning to me as I live Day by day, weeks by week and even into the months, and years. The passed by and it became so intensified and so very apparent that something was almost haunting me although I had heard and seen spirit before, this was different. I had the good Spirits that was helping me telling me not to do the wrong things and then there was the demonic the bad Spirits telling me to do the wrong things it seems demonic in nature to me. It was very depressing and that it reminded me of an evil presence. Even as I fought to go to church, circumstances will come up or lies or excuses I would make just to not go.

Through all this torment there was the fact that I didn't have, not one Bible in the house. This begin to bother me quite a bit and I began a quest to find a Bible. This scared me so much as I felt as if this was the last straw to being in a bad situation in the spiritual realm of things. I hadn't even stopped to think of a Bible not being in the house. I couldn't believe that I didn't have, not one. I felt that there was something evil around me a force that I didn't want to deal with. I had to get closer to God some kind of way and I had to find me a Bible. At this point I set out to buy a Bible I would start to the bookstore to get it but something would happen or change my intentions. I would hear the voice telling me to do something else or buy something else. By the end of the day I would have bought other things or did everything else but buy the Bible that I had left home with intentions of getting in the first place. After going through this aggravation for months it, seemed like months I finally landed a Bible. After much confusion I was able to find a Bible in a surplus store. The Bible had the names of the same number of family members that I had and some of the same names and it was the last name of my family and birth dates. I really I thought that it was put there for me. I looked in amazement at it and I bought it as this was the strangest thing that could have happened it was as if the Spirit of God was there directing me that this was the one to buy.

A sense of relief fell over me, but as it would happen I started having trouble with picking it up and reading it. It was as if I couldn't just pick it up. I would get close to it and sit close to it put it on the end table and sit close to it. I tried placing the Bible on the end table next to the couch because I felt that it would be easier to pick up. I even had problems reading it to begin with. I couldn't remember anything I had read and I would read it over and over again. The bad negitive voice would constantly say "not now do something else" look at TV, play some music, go visit your friends. The good Spirit voice was saying to" pick up the Bible and read it". It was a battle between good and evil it seems as if I was possessed by this evil spirit I wanted to desperately follow the pleasant and good voice that was telling me to read the good book to do the right thing. The temptation was very strong I would cry and pray asking God for strength to do the right thing. At first the temptation was very strong but as time went by I began to have more and more power over the evil voices that I was hearing. These negative voices scared me I could hear the different entities speaking to me about what to do and what not to do, it was very confusing and very uncertain. It didn't seem as though I was myself at all. This was far different than anything I had experienced before in my life. I kept asking God "why is this happening to me? It's as if something evil is there trying to stop me from learning about God and His glory. I knew in my soul that I was a believer and that I had the strength and the belief to pull myself out of this thing and try to evade the situations, to declare war on the spirits that was trying to take hold of my life my mind my body. That's all I could think of at the time. This activity continued for months maybe a year I tried everything I could think of at the time. I had become very desperate to overcome this disturbing forces and what it was doing to me. I was very afraid of whatever was happening to me I wasn't able to sleep hardly at all most nights for weeks at a time in and out things went by my usually getting up in the middle of the night pacing the floor looking for anything to take my mind off of this disturbing situation that was engulfing my world at the time.

Many times I would make plans to go to church on Sunday but by the time that they came I would have made up some kind of excuse or something else that will come into play. I would have started the old trilogy of lying about I had to do something or how it wasn't necessary or that It had nothing to do with whatever was happening to me anymore. I would literally talk or reason with my way out of going to church, because I would have something more important or more interesting to attend to. It was a real push for me to get to church. Finally, I was able to get there but I still had the disturbances of the voices that were ongoing. The friends that I knew and had come in contact with weren't true to their religion so much went on or took place that wasn't right in the church's eyes, but it was always happening at that time. So that wasn't appealing to me either as I was getting mixed up in it too, trying to escape this sort of life was harder yet. Finally, after months of going through so many things like putting the Bible under my pillow at night after I had read it so I could remember what I had read was something else, because I couldn't remember what I had just read. I felt like putting it under my pillow and praying would help me to remember the things and what I remembered started to clear up in my head. At this time I was able to remember verses and understand what I had read.

This made things very real for me after dealing with the forces from the dark side of life, As well as the forces from the good side. Dealing with the spirits of the holy spirit of God has made things very apparent that there is a God in heaven and there are good angels there and here too. It became very real and it brought me closer to my belief in "God" at that time in my life I was experiencing the forces of what can only happen in one's life at the time in life. I have remained constant in the spiritual work of the Holy Spirit and doing my best to learn and study the ways of true religion, and the affects that it can have and in most cases do have are most of us in our everyday lives. It is a fact well known by me and others that through experiences and other realizations that praying and believing, while rebuking the negative spirits, entities, from the other side as well as this side of life and thoughts doing good helping and caring for others and blessing laying on of hands and praying can help us in this life.

Chapter 2

"Oh my God what a ride"

As it would happen another thing happened to me on a cold early winter day. One of those mornings that seemed to come along after there was a few nice warm days. Just enough to fool you into taking off your heavy coats and taking the time to almost feel as if it were Spring already. The weather was brisk and cold for the early morning hours for the day, and after a short weekend with my mother, going to the garden and picking cabbage sprouts and just having a really good time together getting out. Going to the park all was good except while on the drive through the park my sister and I hit a sinkhole in the road. The car bounced out of the hole as I did not see it in time to stop or slow down. The hit was so great that we hit our heads on the top of the interior ceiling of the car. Everything seemed to be okay, so we continued on through the park on to my mother's house for the night. I would usually fill up the gas tank, but I noticed that I still had 3/4 of a tank of gas which was plenty to get me home in the morning. My plans were to leave early enough to get my son some breakfast at Big Boys Restaurant and then drop him off at school. Then I will head on to my classes and then to my part-time job.

As it so happened the ride home was somewhat of a miracle in the making. As we rolled toward home on the expressway many strange things started to happen. The car started to putter and I noticed that we were getting slower and slower I couldn't figure it out everybody and everything was passing us by. The cars were passing us and we were as if moving in slow motion. It was the strangest feeling. The weather was getting worse and raining and it was getting colder and it was a freezing rain. The wind started to blow more. It became darker very fast I could feel the coldness coming through the windows into the car I had the heat on but it seemed like it wasn't working to good. I thought to myself what am I to do now? I was a long way from home this is before they had cell phones and I was way out on the expressway in no man's land. I was a long way from a call box that they used to have on the highway. I don't know if they have them there now or not to make an emergency call to 911. My son was dressed inappropriately no coat or hat just the heat from the car. I had not taken anything to cover up with either. I said to myself "what do I do now? All I could think of was to pray and hope that God will hear my cry for help. As I was in desperate need of all I could do to get home. I prayed with all my might and heart that God will hear me and turn things around for me. There weren't any houses or any type buildings on the way home on the part of the highway that I was traveling. All I could do is pray and ask God for help and getting to a place a safe place a place where I can get some help for my son and myself. At that point the car had stopped. The car has stopped in the middle of the road I became frightened as there could be an accident or something more severe. I was really frightened at this time as my thoughts were that we could really get hurt really bad now. I continue to pray as I sit there in the middle of the road. All at once the car made a great noise like a sirens starting up all at once. I stepped on the gas and the car started to move forward. I had prayed that God would help me get us to a safe place where I can get some help. I wasn't sure how far this was going to take me or if it was going to shut off or down again. The only place I could think of was that there was a lumber yard a head in town on the side of the road not too far ahead. I figured I can make a call there or to get some help. The car roared ahead as we continue down the road toward the lumber yard.

I had named my car Elizabeth affectionately it remind me of a person I used to know that knew exactly what to do at the right time. Elizabeth continued down the highway without any difficulty at all. The ride was smooth as we proceeded toward the lumber yard. I drove through the storm until we reached The lumberyard as soon as I pulled up in the yard the sun came out and the car stopped right there in the driveway. It was as if it was a brand new day. The Sun showed brightly and everywhere everything sparkled in the daylight. It was beautiful it was like a new beginning to the day. I called the insurance company and they said that I didn't have a drop of gasoline in the tank and that it was a miracle that I made it there to the lumberyard. With the weather being as it was, it to me was truly a miracle. Seeing how the weather was. They said that I must have been driving on plain fumes. The insurance guys gave me some gas and checked out the car and I was again on my way for the day. The day was an ordeal but with God's help I made it through. Thank you God it was truly a miracle.

Chapter 3

"Spirit Lifted Me"

Well, after a long period of time I was still living in Grand Rapids, Michigan and trying to make ends meet. I had graduated from college with my bachelor's degree in Allied Health Teacher Education, for dental technology, but could not find a job. It wasn't that there weren't any it was that there were a recession and some prejudice in the field for being a woman and a minority in the field of mostly men. I really love what I was educated to do and I knew that I was very good at it and good with my hands as an artist. I had written to the University of Howard in Washington DC and had secured an interview with the dental tech instructor there for a position as an assistant and instructor in the field. I was dismayed by the conditions I saw in the area of the university and felt unsafe, in the area that I would most likely have to take up residence in until

I could do better. The city, the part I was in was a far cry from what I was used to living in and accustomed to. It was really unkempt, dirty area downtown where I had to come in on the Greyhound bus. The housing looked unkempt and the garbage was all over the place, maybe it was garbage pickup day, but it was scary to me. Everything was piled high in the streets and in the yards. I had never seen anything like that before. The university didn't seem to be too bad after I arrived there with it being in the inner city like that and what I had seen as I was coming in on the bus. I didn't enjoy the trip and the interview was a complete flop to say the least. I think I was just too nervous and disappointed at everything that I had encountered as I was coming into the city. I hadn't really made up my mind it's like it was made up for me. I didn't really feel as if it was a complete loss because I felt that I would be able to do better by some means in the future doing something else. So I returned to Michigan. I looked into other options, things that I could do in relation to people skills and employment. My luck wasn't very well maintained and I had lost a lot of time looking for work. I had promised my friends that I would visit them in a short time, so I was getting desperate to find something some kind of work to just do, to earn the money for the trip. I finally found the job in a clothing company, sewing smuf shirts. This I worked at until I became ill with bronchitis a serious case. I thought I could go back to work but I came down with a second case of it, just as bad as the first. It took a long time to get back to myself. After the illness I decided that I couldn't chance getting sick like that again and I looked for other job opportunities. I finally was introduced to an outfit with a new program by my cousin out of Detroit Michigan. William was his name my cousin was involved in a new corporation called Forever Living Products, which was products made from the Aloe Vera plants. This corporation was just starting up in Michigan. At that time and now it was sold by members called distributors. It hadn't reached the stores yet or the market. We worked for ourselves being independent distributors I really enjoyed the work and the arrangements of how the product was sold and distributed. It gave me lots of Independence and much more time to do other things. Talking to the people and clients was the best. It really turned out to be more of a Spiritual Journey with the people that I was involved with then the product. With all the product testimony's and stories I begin to investigate or look into the meanings of what the people were telling me. It seemed amazing it seem like miracles. I found that the Aloe Vera Plant was mentioned in the Bible and it is called the Aloe Tree in the holy bible. The Bible has many references and what it is used for. All the while I was selling more and more and more of the Aloe Vera Product it was a good business, I loved it. People were beginning to tell me more and more stories about what it was doing for them many of them will begin to cry as they told their stories. It was truly turning out to be a miracle full of testimonies of the product and what it did and it's doing for the people. The first thing that people would say is that it didn't taste good but it's palatable. Then they will continue on with their stories and their testimonies. There were so many testimonies and that they were so anxious to tell me about them for instance this particular lady had a bad case of kidney failure. She purchased some Aloe from me, she was a client for some time. I was introduced to her by another person that knew my mother.

This lady wasn't doing well at all. She was on daily dialysis sometime daily and could not walk any longer. She told me she had not gone grocery shopping after a few years and was able to walk through the store and push her own cart. She told me that she had not gone anywhere besides the doctor offices in a number of years. She was using the Aloe Vera for some time, then one morning early she called me. She was crying when she said and I quote "honey why didn't you tell me that the Aloe Vera was going to hurt me? Then she started to laugh and laugh I didn't know what to think at that point. I begin to think, "what have I done? Have I sold something that is harmful to people? "What am I going to do? " What do I say to her now? Just then she said quote " I went to the store and walked and pushed my own basket and this morning. She then proceeded to tell me that her doctor said that she didn't have to have another dialysis treatment for a year from then. Many more people call telling me their stories, their testimonies this I thought is truly a miracle from God things were going good very good before the bottom fell out. The store started making it putting it on the shelves. That was on a Saturday that she had gone to the store shopping so Sunday I went to church.

Spirit led me to church that morning, but the night before I had something astonishing happened to me during the night. While I slept I heard something in my bedroom move. I open my eyes and saw nothing. All of a sudden I felt a very large object go under my head and neck. I then felt a very large arm or something I thought to myself go under my knees. At this point I became nervous and numb not knowing what to think or do. "What could this be? I asked myself. Then I felt this strange powerful force pick me up into the air. It then started to turn me around in a circle in my bedroom. I could see the door and I could see the dresser, also the pictures on the wall as I was being turned around in a circle. Then all of a sudden I heard the voice of the Spirit say and I quote "say" I love you Jesus" At that point, I repeated what to say, and said I love you Jesus". Then the entity placed me back down on my bed as easily as if I was just a feather. So delicate and precious I was laying there I laid there for a few seconds then I made a quick dash for my mother's bedroom. I literally jumped into her bed behind her. She asked me "what had happened? "what's wrong? I told her that a Spirit had picked me up out of the bed turn me around and had laid me back down just as gently as a feather. Her reply was "why you come in here? What makes you think that the spirit won't come in here and do the same thing". I thought that makes sense, so I went back to my bedroom and eventually I fell asleep.

After getting to church that following morning I sat next to Reverend Buchanan he was known to be one of the better mediums in the church. He looked at me very strangely and said "what did you do? You must have done something very good? Spirit of God is very happy with you God sent His Angels to let you know that he is pleased with you. To tell the truth that is all the approval that I needed to know that God has His hands and everything on Earth and I do love the feeling. Although at first it unnerved me quite a bit being picked up that way, but I know it had to be the spirit of the almighty God and His Angels and that I can relish for the continuance of my life, thank you Lord.

Chapter 4

"You know not How I Come"

It was in the late 1990s, it was so cold during the early winter months. I was living in Lansing, Michigan. I was just an hour and a half drive from my mother's in Grand Rapids, Michigan. On the weekends I would usually drive or take the Greyhound Bus or my husband would take me to my mother's, which once there we would go to the garden go rummaging, pick vegetables go to sales and pick some things to can for the winter months. This time of the year was late fall almost winter so it was very cold quite cold no snow but cold. I had made it to my mother's house in Grand Rapids, Michigan. The night before the event we had decided to go to an estate sale before we went picking in the gardens. I was running a little late to the estate sales which had started already about 8:00 a.m.

Mother had finished what she was doing and was

dressed and ready waiting in the car in the driveway for me at the back of the house. We were going to the sales in East Grand Rapids, that's where the best sales were we figured. We were excited as to what we would find for a bargain in those days it depended on the part of town you went to and the bargains you got were different than most. Mother had got in the car in the driveway waiting for me to come out, so we could go to the sale we were excited about what we were going to find. I had just got my my coat on and my hat to go to the back door and get in the car when all of a sudden the front doorbell ranged. I didn't want to stop what I was doing but I hesitated and decided to go back through the house to the front door again. I went in to the living room to answer the doorbell,

As I approach the door a strange feeling flowed over me. Opening the door I saw a well-built Caucasian man with a small statue and wearing a large brown oversized coat. I asked him what he needed or wanted and at that very instant I heard a voice over the top of my head and I quote it was a loud spoken voice and it said "you know not how I come" it was as if the voice of the Holy Spirit was speaking to me. The man continued to hold out his hand which he had some change in his hand. I told him no thanks I don't want your money. He said can you spare me some food to eat? and I said "yes" I told him to wait a minute I'll get you something to eat. I headed for the kitchen. I made him a sandwich apple pie, juice etc... And something to carry it in, I took it to him, he said thank you and turn to leave. I told him he could sit here but when I looked again he was gone. My mother and I looked up and down the streets, when I told her what had happened, but we could not find him. Where could he have gone so quickly caring so much? There weren't any cars parked on the street. Where could he have gone and who was he "God".

I have often wondered that I may have found out more about the man at the door that morning if I had only taken the time to think about what the spiritual voice has said to me. That morning we were always in such a hurry to do other things instead of paying closer attention to what is really going on and happening to us and around us at a given time. We miss out on so much by being inattentive. I am so glad that I at least know and have faith enough to help my fellow man, because I would have been in despair for the rest of my life knowing that I had let the Angels of God go by without even knowing that they the Angels do exist in our lives. At this period in time I feel as if I have experienced a wonderful coming of the Holy Spirit.

Chapter 5

"Let the Story be Told,
the Challenger"

This event really interests me because there was an African-American involved a, man. I had been following it for some time then all at once Spirit began to nudge me on about going to the Spiritualist Temple in Santa Monica, California. I live downtown Los Angeles quite a ways from the Temple in Santa Monica. It would take me a couple hours to get there on the bus. So I was somewhat hesitant about going. I remember it being around the end of November when I went on a Sunday. I was very much urged by spirit to go. I was told by Michael's aunt that he would be there and it would be something unusual. What, I didn't know but I wanted to see Michael, the spiritual prophet. Thinking more about my own desire to have my reading done by Michael as I had waited so long to get in touch with him, I just knew it was going to be something that would truly benefit me. At last I will get to have a private reading from Michael and find out what will be in the stars for me. So I made my plans and went with my son to Santa Monica to the Temple.

It was some kind of a day it was beautiful sun shining when we arrived. I was a little late getting to the Temple. I left my son at the cafe down the street, a couple of doors down from the temple he wanted something to eat. I went into the Temple to get the message from Michael. I opened the door to the Temple and to my surprise the room was filled with reporters and a lot of other people that I had never seen before. They had cameras and notebooks and notepads and tape recorders. "What is this all about I ask myself". Soon Michael came out and took his place at the podium. As he stood there I wondered to myself. "Dear God what is going on today here and now? So Michael began to talk. He said he had some news that was very important for the world to know, and that he would not be giving messages at that time, my heart fail to my feet. He said that he would be giving messages at a later time and he would talk to whoever needed to get one at the end of the report.

The report began a bit unusual. Michael stated that several nights before he was in his bed when the entities appeared to him. They told him that it was very important to let the people know that there will be a terrible catastrophe that could be prevented. If it was taken care of before the shuttle is to be lunch in

January. The entity stated that it will not be taken care of or fixed beforehand. As we are here to warn the world of this even. They continued to say that there is a crack in the ring of the panel of the shuttle. The reporters and the people listened and took the information in the service with them when it was over. Time went by about a month or so, and I decided to make the trip to my father's home in West Virginia. Looking at the news each day and following the topics on the Challenger shuttle. It was reported to officials of the news about the shuttle aircraft going to outer space and was very interesting. It seemed like the whole world was waiting for the flight to take place.

On Tuesday January 28th 1986 I was busy cleaning house and getting ready for lunch. When over the television, on most channels the world was getting ready for the takeoff of the challenger. I took the time for a sit-down break to watch the news on the television set. It was just a few minutes from the time for the shuttle to begin the takeoff. Just as I got settled with things and in place I was looking at the shuttle go up, up, up, into the sky and to the amazement of the world there was a huge blast and blaze in the atmosphere. The Shuttle, Challenger had just blown up. My eyes left the TV set and I looked at my watch. It was the exact time the entities had said it would be when it happened. Eastern Standard Time, 11:38a.m.which was the exact time given by the entities.

The entities told Michael to tell us that they have lived here amongst us for a long time and that they can be in any different image. That they are able to come and go through the universe as they wish, whenever and however they wish. As time went by after the shuttle exploded there was much discussion as to whether or not it was known or that it could have been avoided or was it an error in judgment or what?. The question was what could have gone wrong? It was much discussion about what had happened and who was at blame. The entities said that the truth would eventually come out into the open. That, at first they, who were in charge, would deny it but it, the truth would eventually come out for the world to know. The entities came to let Michael warn the people of the devastation. This could have been avoided if only certain people in charge would have listened to the voices of the masters of the universe. Or what they can do and that things do occur when people don't pay attention to what the spirits and entities in the universe have to help them with. If we had only had the ability and the understanding, with open minds to acknowledge that there are Spirits and Angels of God that knows more and do more than we do here on Earth, these things can be avoided.

Chapter 6

"The Stranger in my Life"

Early in the fall after I had completed my Bachelor's Degree from collage I met a guy named Bruce. I was told by the medium that I saw at the church that I would meet some man by this first name. So when it happened, I was somewhat taken by his unusual kindness his devotion to my son and being so helpful to my mother. At that time, I had never met anyone that acted in such a way. It wasn't love at first sight but I grew quite fond of him. I begin to think of him as my protector, someone for the first time in my life that I could depend on. I really admire him for the things that he did and was capable of doing. He had a good job with the state and he was an army man having served and being in the National Guard. I became very proud of him and the things he did. At first I thought we got along very well except for two things. He was very possessive and he didn't talk much and that bothered me. As it happens I was the talker in our conversations. I was also told this by the medium but I figured I could change that in time and time will change things. Time went by and what I thought would work its way out didn't and things began to be more and more strained. I noticed things changing in his attitude but I didn't know why at that time. Then I later realized when my son's father would come to visit him. He would act out of sorts; mean if you can call it that. Things had become very difficult. One day I asked Bruce if I could use the car to go for an interview. The night before for the following day which was Monday. He said that it would be okay and that he would bring the car to me and that he would walk the short distance from where I live to his work. He did bring the car over the next morning, but he did something to it. My son was on his way to school. I thought my son was at school by the time he returned back to the house and said that Bruce was taking something out of the car, and that he didn't put anything back in it. By that time Bruce had left for his job walking. I looked at Derrick and said of course he had to put some fluid back in the car because he just brought me the keys and said everything was all right now and that I can take it. At that point my son "said that he didn't put anything back in the car". I was sure that there was a mistake. My son again left for school and I continued to get dressed for my interview that morning.

On my way to the interview everything went

smoothly, but I kept thinking about Derrick coming back to the house to tell me Bruce didn't put anything back in the car. I got to thinking that Derrick probably was mistaken or that Bruce was just messing with the windows or the fluid or something else at the time. That he was Just checking things out for me. I continue on to the interview. The interview went well it was lunch time at about 12:00 when the traffic is rushing and heavy. I hate it driving in that type of traffic I dreaded it. I would have to take the same route to get back home, but I had no choice the only way to get back was to drive the same route back. I had prayed to build up my dexterity and nerves to make the trip back home especially after what I had been thinking earlier about Bruce and the car. I had entered Stocking Avenue one of the busiest streets in Grand Rapids especially at lunch time and at 5:00 p.m. it was a hilly avenue going straight downhill, cars parked on the street. As I started to turn onto the avenue the car speed it up as I proceeded. I found myself going faster and faster I pressed the brakes there was nothing. I pressed again still no signs of the brakes catching as I floated downhill like the wind at a very high speed. I pumped the brakes still there was nothing "Oh my God my brakes are gone "Oh my God help me" how am I going to stop this car from flying down this hilly avenue? I prayed and called on God again and again God answered me. I went through several red lights and there weren't any cars on the road. As I came to the end of the avenue I took the turn on it felt like one wheel as I floated down the road. As I proceeded on down the road I asked God what to do to stop the car? All at once as I pulled up into the gas station lots of power coming from the car as I spread past the gas station entrance, I was scared. I heard the voice say "take the keys out" I pulled the keys out and the car stopped halted just as I was approaching the back fence of the gas station at the top of the Hill. Everything, everything filled with white smoke I couldn't see a thing. The service men ran out yelling "What in the world is happening" What happened they asked me? The men checked out the car. They told me that there was no brake fluid in the car. I was so upset I hadn't even noticed the lights on the dashboard. I didn't see any or I just didn't remember seeing any.

After all a lot of things were happening in the family that I couldn't make heads or tails of and Bruce denied having anything to do with the car that morning. I found it hard to believe but my doubt set in I was going through many changes at the time. Bruce said that it had to have been in my head for that to happen nothing was wrong with the car. I didn't know what to do I just prayed a lot and I said things should get better I don't know if Derrick had made a mistake or not but Bruce denied having anything to do with any brake fluid. Bruce swore that he hadn't do anything like that so I kind of went along with it praying that I wasn't making a mistake with my son. Bruce was doing a lot of things to help the family so I didn't want to make waves I wanted to believe that he would not do such a thing why would he? I couldn't think of any reason. I began to become very suspicious as time went by and other happenings would take place with Bruce. I just couldn't wrap my mind around it so to get over it all I decided to move away so the incidences would stop happening. It would be years before I really found out what type of man he was and what he had planned to do to me.

As I have moved thousand miles away from him and those accidents or activities as they were called had stopped I felt more compelled to be my own person. I thought that moving away would help me in getting out of whatever was happening so I moved to beautiful sunny California. With God's help I was able to get my funds together and my son and I moved. Things were working out pretty good as we lived in Los Angeles. I was there for 2 years. I started over again with the help of God but that didn't last for too long because I had to return back to Michigan to get the help for my son, as he was under age.

While I was living in California I worked with an agency. I had found a good job working as an assistant to a well-off businessman and his wife. It was very nice I was enjoying myself. The gentleman was the maker of greeting cards. He was from Europe and had lots of prestigious friends. He was involved with quite a few presidents in his time. I really enjoyed listening to his stories about his life and the things he did Mr. Shucart was retired for many years and had a wife Jeanette and a daughter Nancy who lived nearby with her family in Beverly Hills, California, Things took a turn because I was doing too much and became over stressed. it is true that stress will kill you. I'm a good example of it. I became very ill from stress related illness I had to return back to Grand Rapids, Michigan to seek help for me and my son. As my son was underage and needed someone to care for him. That happened to be my mother's good nature, that's all I had to depend on. So that's how I ended up back in Michigan because of necessity. I went on to West Virginia after I dropped my son off in Michigan at my mother's. I thought that it would be a good place to take a break and a rest to pull my nerves together. I stayed and improved on my health for several months, then decided to return to Grand Rapids, Michigan to be with my son and family. This was the beginning of the end of Bruce and his relationship with me as he decided to do things that I couldn't even imagine a person would want to harm me in this way. I often wondered who would want to harm me and I couldn't come up with anyone except for the things that Bruce would do to me. I remembered Ms. Amante telling me that what this man has planned for me God will not let it work and God will take him before he got a chance to do what he had planned, I found that unbelievable since I had did nothing, had hurt no one. I found myself watching the people that I hung out with or had been around. It was just unbelievable that someone would want to do me harm. I couldn't see it in his actions. He was always doing something to appease me. Now that all of this has happened to me I can understand how so many women, young girls, older women wind up hurt and in dire situations, because of some men in relationships. Most of the time we can't see the problem or incidence coming our way, when it's so close to us. It's mainly the people on the outside they see it first. All in all I thank God for the mediums that He put in this world on this Earth to help us and guide us. If we would only listen to the true mediums and Prophets that God has placed here for us we would do a lot better for ourselves.

Chapter 7

"Spiritual Visitor During The Night"

Some years ago, I had a problem with my breast. Every year the mammogram would come back showing a dense spot on the x-ray. This continued for some years when I was in my mid 30s and 40s. I was quite worried that it may turn malignant at some point in the future. But every year I went to the doctors, they didn't do anything about it. That is the mass in my breast. As the years went by I became very curious of what it is and the news and the publicity around breast cancer. While I went to the spiritualist church most of the time to get news of what may be in my future. I was told at that time in my 40s that Spirit visitors would visit me during the night to help.

I had finally found the doctor that saw the mass to be abnormal after so many years. My doctor sent me to make an appointment for surgery. The morning of the surgery in the wee hours of the morning something very amazing was happening in my home in my bedroom. Every morning for about 3 weeks I would wake up and my mattress would be almost halfway off my bed. During the night I will hear the house settling and the stairs creeping as if someone was climbing up them. This particular night of my surgery Spirit woke me up and I saw a being or entity at the side of my bed. The entity was just standing there looking at me. I stared at the being for about 20 seconds then I said to the being "what are you doing here? and "what do you want? "What's going on? Than the entity, being raised its hand as if to wave. The being told me that everything would be all right. At that point the entity flashed out of sight. I couldn't go back to sleep as I had to get up to get ready for my appointment at the hospital, to have the surgery on my breast.

I hurry to the hospital to keep my appointment. When I arrived I was fitted with my gown and given my pills for the operation to take place. The tech, the X-ray person, took the needle the x-rays but could not find any abnormal mass in my breast. He was told to take them again, and again they came back with nothing. He must have taken about 12 of them the surgeon came in to check me and to check the x-rays but could not find any abnormalities. Then two more doctors came in to view and examine the x-rays again nothing. They said they have to have the X-ray machine checked out and tested so they did that. The report came back that there was nothing wrong with the machine. Once again they took the last two X-rays, 13 I believe in all. The doctors, said that they could not find it at that point there's nothing to be done and they said I had to go home, but Dr. Soso said that he knew that I had been praying a lot and that it has to be a miracle. He told me that he was going to follow up with me with this for some time to come, which he did. He called me about every month for about a year. I don't understand it but I do know that all these happenings are the work of the Spirit of God and His Angels. Till this day I have had no occurrences or abnormalities found in my breast I take my mammogram every year and they have been normal. Thanks to the Holy Spirit.

Chapter 8

"Grandma Mary's Visit"

It was the middle of October so many years ago. Spirit was really working with me and helping me focus on things spiritually. I had been having many visions and a lot of happenings. I was constantly saving what little money I could. Not buying many things that I needed at certain times as I just was working part-time as a substitute teacher. Things were somewhat tight for us as my husband had made some bad investments in property and other things; he had trusted people to do for him. I was having all sorts of dreams and visions at the time, about everything you might imagine.

One morning as I was waking up, just lying there thinking about what to do for the day. I heard a female voice saying "Today is Mommy's Day" I immediately looked in the direction of the voice and saw a small light skin woman with long hair gathered in a ball on top of her head. She was wearing a long dress and a long white apron. Her hair was up on her head in a ball and it was snow white. I said to myself "what or who is this? then she repeated herself saying "Today is Mommy's Day" she just stood there holding the money in her hands it seem like it was the turn of the century dollars in both her hands they were different colors and very large. I had never seen these before they were larger than what we have now and we're in different colors. In answer to my question, is that the conclusion I came to was this must be someone in the family. is that this was a grandmother that I had not met before. I had become excited as I looked her up and down noticing her garb and dressing as I kept saying to myself "what does she mean that "Today is Mommy's Day? I couldn't think of anyone's birthday at that particular time. Not my mother's nor my grandmother's, birthdays were at that same time of the year or month. Whatever, it made me very excited and I felt that she was giving me a message to go out and do some shopping for things that I hadn't got in some time.

I had a thought that because she said Mommy that maybe it had to do with my mother. So I called my mother before I took off shopping to see if she could figure it all out. Mother asked me "what the spirit look like." I told mother that she looked like she was or may have been an Indian woman. Mother said that the spirit was her grandmother Mary who was a small woman with Snow White hair as I had described her. I told mother that she had money in her hands and that I didn't know what that meant, except to spend some of it or to play the lottery that day. I thought we had decided to play the lottery because mother said that her, Grandma Mary's name played for in the lottery for a certain number. So I thought mother was going to play it that day and we finished talking and hung up the phone. I went on and did my shopping not thinking about the lottery anymore that day. I just knew mother had played it and had some luck. It took me several trips back and forth to the house with my shopping, before I was through for the day. My husband looked at me with such amazement when I told him how good I felt getting everything taken care of that morning. He just kept asking me "where are you going? "where you going? "where you going now? I just said that I'll be back and I was off again. As night settled in I got ready for bed feeling as if I had done a great big deal for the day. I was very satisfied and happy that I had taken care of a lot of things that I had put off for a long time, I had finally got it done. Just as I had gotten ready to settle in for the night, the phone began to ring.

The telephone rang just then and I answered it. It was my mother very excited she asked. Did I get the number? I said that I didn't get the number I said "did you get the number? I told her that I hadn't played the lottery. She said you didn't play? She said that the number came out it was Mary mother hadn't played it either. That wasn't the first time that that had happened. It had been several times as Spirit had entered our lives to give us a helping hand. You have to take it for what it's worth at the time and act on it. The Holy Spirit is always there to help when the need arises.

Chapter 1

"Out of The Mouths of Babs"

Sometime ago I had promised my friends that I went to college with, they live overseas iñ the Caribbean. I told them that I would be over for a visit in a couple of years. Time has passed by rather quickly, with my not having a full-time job. I was doing the Aloe Vera Products, selling distributorship, but that wasn't much at the time. Sales had started to drop off, after it had hit the market. So that made things a bit difficult for me. On top of the sales dwindling we were in a recession at the time. So it took some time to get my ticket. I finally was able to receive the ticket and save some money by working in a clothing company for some time before my trip. I had a lot of plans as to what to do and have some fun getting together with my friends to do things again. After such a solemn two and a half years of having to bounce around from job to job. I caught a severe case of having a severe case of bronchitis. After thinking about changing job for such a long time I decided now was the time for me to make a change.

While planning for my trip I worried a lot about my son and if he would be okay staying with my mother, as she was getting older and he was very mobile and at that age of exploring and doing his own thing. He was getting older and trying to do things his way. I would attend the church regularly to get some answers to what was bothering me. As time went by the speakers would give me information on my life and my son's life. Reverend John Gray who came to the church with James Edwards who are great spiritualist mediums was regulars at the church in Grand Rapids, Michigan. Sylvia Brown was also a much highlighted medium that came there also. This one particular Church day when Reverend John Gray was to guest speak. He was especially good at billets. This is where he asked the participants to write down questions that they need answered on a piece of paper and put it into a container mixed up. The container is given to Reverend Gray and he picks up a piece of paper and or note and reads the questions and answers it for the participant. He gives them the answer and ask whose it is and if it was correct or not. He was always right on the nose. I asked the most important question of all that I had that day. That was "will my son be safe on his oversized bicycle? Because, this concerned me the most, with the traffic on the roads and him getting in the streets on his bike I was very worried. Reverend John Gray said that my son would be taken care of and watched over very well while I was gone on my vacation. Reverend Gray said The Holy Spirit and the Angels would watch over him for me and he would be safe. My son will tell me all about it when I return from my trip.

I was gone for a month, the trip turned out okay. I enjoyed my visit. Almost every other day I had to call to see about him and how things were with mother. I wondered what Derrick was going to tell me, what it would be all about? I made the long trip home. I settled in to talk to my mother about the trip. She told me that he was okay but he wouldn't sleep in his bedroom. My mother said that Derrick would come into her bedroom every night. He would not sleep in his bedroom!! She said that Derrick kept coming into her bedroom sleeping on the floor by her bed every night. She would see him there when she woke up in the mornings. I asked myself "what could have been wrong that he wouldn't stay in his own bedroom in his bed? I wonder "what had happened? At that point Derrick came into the house. He hugged me and whispered in my ear, that he thinks that he is going crazy. I looked at him and he looked so confused, as if he didn't know what to think or do. He was just 8 years old at the time. I hugged him back and told him to tell me what had happened "what did you see? "What happened honey?

Derrick began to tell me all about the things that happened while I was away. My son said that every night that I was gone my Indian guide came to watch him. The Indian stood in the doorway of the bedroom and watched him with his back to Derrick. Then he told me about two people a tall man a tall skinny man and a short lady with long hair and they had a little dog. Every night they would come also and watch over him and he saw them go down the steps. The Indian would make a loud thumping noise when he came and would wake Derrick up he said. The tall man and woman would look at him and go down the stairs with the little dog. I know who the Indian is, but I didn't know about the man and the woman except for what I had heard in the past. When my mother heard that about the man the tall thin man and the short woman with the long hair. She literally jumped up saying "how could he know anything about them and that they had a little dog? and they really did, my mother said. My mother said that those two people the tall thin man and the little short woman with the long hair was her grandparents.

Her grandfather was tall and thin and her grandmother was short with long hair, long white hair and they had a little dog she remembered them vividly. I've had numerous exposures to the mediums living in this spiritual world. It's been wonderful to experience the meaning of life after death. I've been in contact with entities from the other side who are relatives. The spiritual entities can come back into one's life to help guide us and even help to heal those that we love in this lifetime. My son had asked who they were I told him that they were spiritual entities from the other side, and that I had prayed to God for them to come and watch over him for me while I was away. I was worried about him getting into an accident with his bike. I also asked that God and His Angels take care of him in this life and the next.

I didn't realize that my son was so spiritual he has given me advice in the past that has come true or became factual. Also I'm beginning to believe that this may actually run in the family. He was so young when these incidences happened to him. I believe it's like that with most of us, things happen as we are young and we just don't remember when we get older, or we don't remember much about them after a while. This is another reason why my faith is concrete in the spiritual world. I am so grateful for having so many associates that believe in the spiritual life in this world and are in my life.

Chapter 10

"Inception, the Story of Myra"

This story is about Myra a dear friend of mine. Myra was an adopted child; she was adopted at about age 1 year old. She did not know who her parents were, her biological parent, that is. Myra was adopted by a young couple who were teachers. They did pretty well for themselves. They lived in the suburbs of Atlanta, Georgia. Myra was the only child in the family. She had much of what she needed and wanted in life as a child and a teenager. When Myra was in the 11th grade in high school she was awarded a new car on her birthday. This was for her diligence in school and her devotion to her parents. She went to college and was very devoted to her studies. She had a pretty simple non-complicated life at that time. After her fourth year of education Myra stayed at college, at which time she was in the nursing program. Myra graduated and began a new job at the area hospital. She worked there for several years and met a guy by the name of Ned. She and Ned fell in love almost immediately. They worked and planned a family together which started about a year or so after marriage. They raised two young men together. After a while things appeared to turn sour for the couple.

Myra found out that Ned had two children by other women. This hurt Myra so deeply the insult, the dishonesty, the lies. It was as if she had been living in an imaginary world for all her married life. This was unbelievable and unbearable and so very hard for Myra to wrap her mind around. She suffered the embarrassment of the feelings of loss. People and friends alike gossiped behind her back. The whole gambit was too much for her to take Myra finally filed for a divorce.

It took some time, years if you will, to come to a resolve over it. But what else could she really do? After all she thought she wasn't the only woman this has happened to. Myra thought to herself. "I'll bet that there have been millions of women going through the same thing. She said to herself, "that's right "get a grip girl, "get back up on your feet". So time went by Myra again begin to function like herself. Things were going good, very good. Then one day she felt badly at work. This went on for some time. For a period of about a year she just didn't feel like herself. She began to have or experience a weakness, tired and she had vision problems. She felt that her balance was off too. Myra thought that maybe she should see a doctor. The vitamins weren't helping that she had been taking to give her more energy. Eventually Myra went to the doctor for a test. She took test after test. Finally the results came back. Myra had contracted Ms., multiple sclerosis, Myra was given an advanced stage of the disease, she had told me.

When I met Myra, we weren't introduced or anything like that. I was sitting outside the clubhouse where we lived. Just enjoying the weather that day as I had done on so many days, when there wasn't much to do. I would just go out to watch people. Pass the time of the day, say hi to a few friends etc…, and discuss the weather and so on, just a typical day. Sitting there one day I noticed this lady in a wheelchair on her way to the mailbox. I would see her about every 2 days. She must be a new resident" I thought to myself" because I hadn't seen her here at the complex before. I saw her going to the mailbox almost every two days. As I watched her push yourself along to home, I felt that I should have said something. Spirit spoke to me saying "she's going to walk again". I didn't know anything about this woman before seeing her coming and going to the mailboxes. I questioned myself as to why I would even think such a thing. Spirit started urging me to tell her that she will be all right and that she was going to walk again. It got to the point that every time I saw her Spirit was urging me to talk with her and what to say. I was thinking about it even when I didn't see her out and about.

I said to myself" how would I approach a person like her in a wheelchair and tell them they are going to walk again"? Well the time came one day I was sitting out at the clubhouse, when she came out and was on her way to the mailbox. I looked at her and with the continuous nudging from Spirit I then decided I would say something to her that day. She got her mail and continued around the building till she was out of my sight. I thought I had to make it another day now. I thought I had lost my courage. So I decided to go to my apartment. Walking by the buildings I said to myself that I should have said something to stop her as I was almost to my building. Turning the corner I saw her sitting under one of the trees in the shade. She was just sitting there in her wheelchair alone. Spirit said to me "say it now". I walked up to her and introduced myself and I said to her that I have something to tell you. I asked if it was all right if I talk to her about her illness. She shook her head and said yes. First I explained to her that I wasn't a kouk or nut or anything like that. I'm a Spiritualist. I then told her it may sound strange to you but the Spirit of God wants me to tell you that "you will be okay, all right and that you will walk and even run again". At that point I began to prophesy to her about what the Spirit of God was showing me about her future, and some things that had happened in the past. She agreed to what I was saying and we exchanged contact information. I said God bless you. She thanked me and she smiled and I returned to my apartment

Soon I received a call from Myra asking how I was doing and she wanted to know how long I had been doing readings. I told her that it has been many, many years and I asked her if she had heard about the different camps for Spiritualists in Orlando. She said no and that she hadn't heard of Spiritualists either. Well we talked and I told her more of what the Spirit of God had told me to say. That was the beginning of our relationship. Time went by and we had conversations about most everything and concerns she had about her family. Especially her second son to the oldest son he was on drugs pretty bad and she couldn't do anything to help him. He eventually got killed by someone. Myra grieved and moved on with her life. In the meantime Myra was having her own issues with her Ms. She decided to take a class in phlebotomy and was doing very well. She had passing grades, at an exceptional level. The only thing was she could not stand to take the practice exam, for drawing the blood from the patient. She could take that at a later date because, I was sure she would be able to stand then, because the Spirit of God had told me so.

Not long after this concern with not sanding Myra had an incident with the bus driver picking her up to take her home. He stepped up to her one day as she was being lifted on the bus, and said to her "what do you think you're doing here? You can't do that kind of work. This broke her heart and she called me crying over the phone. I prayed with her and told her not to let the devil take her Joy. And we pray more to ward off the evil vibes the bus driver tried to put into her mind.

As Myra would go and come from her classes. There were a lot of watchable eyes and murmuring about her, believing what I had told her about being able to walk again. The people would watch and some would even laugh at her, Myra told me. I told her to just ignore them because that was just their ignorance in them and that they were non-believers. Myra said that there was a lot of hurt coming from people around her. she didn't give up she kept going and we kept praying. I told Myra that they didn't have the beliefs and faith in themselves or God to try to get out of their own situation. Other instances follow and she was able to handle them much better as we pray together almost every night and day.

The mere idea of negativity was against her capacity for survival. She completed all but the clinical, and concentrated on continuing to get better health wise. Later that month I had a vision while I slept about her sitting up in her bed with her legs pumped up. I called her that morning and asked if she was sitting up at the moment with her legs pulled up to her chest. She started to laugh and she said "yes I am right now", about 3 days later she called me and said that she was able to stand up in front of the walker, at about 3:00 a.m. in the morning I got a call from her. She told me that she was standing up in front of the bed. Next said she was at the kitchen sink just standing there, that she had walked there from her bedroom on her own. Myra was so excited she said that she wanted to scream I told her to scream and scream because you have had a miracle happen to you. Myra started to scream. Everyone had to hear in the building. I told her to scream and give God the Glory he deserves, because you have been healed today. Myra continued to improve with her exercises and treatment that she was getting from her doctor.

Myra continued to improve and got a job that she had found in the mall.

She joined the gym and got with the coach doing very well. Many people stood in her way and said it couldn't be done, but with her strength in God she is pulling though.

The idea that Myra believed in me made me more of a believer than I had been in the past. So many experiences and so much doubt was there at first when I started with Myra, but now I know in my heart that Myra will accomplish her goals. Be able to play ball, run and do the things that she want to accomplish in this life. She realized that it was her faith in God and His Spirits that made all these things possible for her to grow and progress as she has. She truly believed I know she does with every pour in her body, that it is just the force of God that is guiding her today thank you God. Today Myra is doing quite well she's working she's driving she's traveling she's being Myra thank God for that.

Chapter 11

"Million Doller Plot Spoiled"

Not long after my marriage to Bruce it became apparent that there were things or happenings that had taken place in the pass years that I wasn't aware of at the time. Many happenings that I had been told were a figment of my imagination, or something even more bizarre to me or was only in my mind. Things started to become clear to me and made me scared. I started to remember incidents that had happened and things that I hadn't realized had really happened at the time. I was overwhelmed by life at that time. So many things were happening that I couldn't phantom that it could possibly be Bruce. This had to be the one person whom I had turned to as my protector, and my mate. The one who cared for me, or I thought. As time went by years to be exact I begin to notice things in his attitude and behavior. He was heavily in debt at the time for making some foolish property arrangements with people that he wasn't acquainted with at the time. He was, I found out in need of money. The house and car payments were going lacking along with other things. I tried to do what I could but I had my own bills.

After work one afternoon I was let off early, I continued on home. Had started dinner when the phone ringed. I thought to myself that it had to be for Bruce because I didn't get that many calls, but I had made it home before him so I just answered it. I said hello, there was a gentleman on the other end. Who stated that he was from the insurance company. He then stated that he had another form that had to be filled out as soon as possible, in order to make the contract active. He said that he was sorry for calling but the form wasn't with the completed five. The gentleman continued to say that when we were in the office he didn't have it at that time. I asked him "when were we in the office? He repeated "yes you and your husband a few days ago. I asked what type of insurance policy is it ? It's the million dollar policy on you that your husband and you took out the day of your visit. I told the man thank you and hung up the phone. I couldn't believe my ears. I had never been to an insurance office with my husband. It must be a mistake on the agents' part. If my husband had been to that insurance office who was the woman passing as me, his wife? This produced new questions of concern about Bruce and other things that I thought was a figment of my imagination. I just couldn't believe what was happening. "Why would he take out a million dollar policy on me and nothing on himself"? What were his intentions? I didn't have any health problems to really speak of except for being overweight about 30 lbs. The only conclusion I could come up with was that he may be thinking or planning for my demise. And "who was the woman that went with him to the insurance company? I thought about it over and over again I could only think of one person that it could be his, sister, Naomi she was built much like myself and about my age. Hair was about the same color too. She and Bruce were very close in age and also in relationships as siblings. I overheard them at times sharing secrets before, and discussing them. So it came to reason that she would be the one most likely to have gone with him to the insurance office. I still didn't know for sure but it made plenty of sense to me at that time. This would become clear later in a matter of a short period of time. I confronted Bruce with what I knew and what I was told by the agent at the insurance company. I asked "who he took with him and why her and not me? What was that for? He never answered my questions.

She had made a statement one day when she called and as I had answered the phone. She said that quote "everyone would get what they are due real soon". I couldn't imagine what she was talking about at the time, but now it makes sense. I thought to myself what is wrong with these people? What kind of mess have I gotten myself involved with now dear God help me?

I just had to guess at it all for a while. I prayed and I asked the Holy Spirit of God "what and why"? Dear

God I need your help I'm trying to deciding what to do next. I decided to tell Bruce what the Profit Reverend Sagest had told me some time ago, about him and his mother having had part in my being done the way I have been treated by the police, at the time in the past. When they would just come to wherever I was and pick me up for no reason and take me to the mental health hospital in Grand Rapids, Michigan this had happened several times. The police would take me to the hospital there for no reason. They would ask me "who I was? "Where did I live? "What do you do? They told me that I had to live with my mother and I couldn't stay anywhere else. One time they picked me up and they tried to put a gun into my purse, but it wouldn't fit, my purse was too small. they had it in the police car trunk.

I had my own apartment at the time so I didn't know what it was all about. The police would take off their badges and drive me around the city with the lights on inside the car. That particular evening I was at my childhood friend's house just having a nice time talking about old times, classmates and just having a good time talking and enjoying each other's company. When Bruce showed up I wasn't ready to leave, and had decided to stay a little longer, I told him and then he left. Next thing we knew there was a knock on the door and the police pulled me out. Just like that, we couldn't imagine what had happened. I was at a loss for understanding. I had no idea who or what was happening or who was behind it. This had happened before to me after Bruce was around and had left. Not my friend or myself could figure out what was happening and why. Diane and I had known each other since grade school and have always stayed in contact with each other. This is all happening in the city of Grand Rapids, Michigan.

I believe that I had to stand still and have faith that God will make it all right in the end. God has cleared up many disturbances that happened in the past years. I know now to hang on and believe in God and his words and things will turn out in a way one wouldn't imagine. I love you God, for all you have done for me and all that you have planned for my future. Thank you for giving me all that you have with my faith I know I will not be disappointed

I had no idea what was going on and who was behind it all for years. It all became clear one day as Bruce's sister came to visit him. They were going out of town on some kind of business. Bruce was shocked that I had been told that by Reverend Sagest years ago. He had run out of the house. I went upstairs and saw him standing behind his van just looking at the house like he was scared of something.

Since I had met Bruce my life was more like a roller coaster upside down so much of the time. From the beginning it seems so unreal. The things that would happen and I would ask "why? But there wouldn't be any reply back from him. I found over the years that his thinking was way different than mine. He didn't appear to be normal, I mean that he acted very strange at times, which I feel was one of the reasons we had such a difficult time communicating. This just made things more complicated in our relationship. I was a nervous wreck most of the time while living with him. I believe that he boarder lined on unstable and jealousy. As far as I was concerned that was it, that was all there was to it. As time went by things just became worse. And as time went by I began to be more and more afraid of what he would or would not do to me. After all that I had found out about the thing that had happened in my life as I had known him over the years. I begin to put things or incidences together. It was very hard for me to imagine a person doing these things to me. Someone who I had grown to trust and believe in, would actually plan to harm me for money, of all things I thought. As I had seen things before concerning Bruce's attitude, what I was told shocked me deeply. I had never met anyone that would do these types of things to a person. Even though I had heard of people doing far worse things to their fellow men, I never thought it would happen to me. It was like having a nightmare or living through one.

I was out of work and had gone to visit my friend Gerda who lived around the corner. I had known her for quite a few years but this day I decided to go home and take a nap. While I was there in the bed trying to rest they came in. I heard them talking about me. They didn't know I was upstairs as I had left my car around the corner at Gerda's house and walked home. All of a sudden I heard his sister say talking to Bruce when all of a sudden she asked him "what are you going to do now Bruce? I didn't hear what Bruce said but I did hear her, Naomi, say that they're not going to keep her then "what are you going to do next? At this point I knew that I couldn't depend on my own understanding of what was happening. I had to get away from this family at all costs. I just prayed to God for help and plan my getaway. I remained quiet until they left and prayed that he wouldn't come upstairs. My car was parked at Gerda's house and I had walked around the corner from her house so they didn't see my car or figure that I was at the house. As soon as they left I rushed and packed my car up with all that I could take so I wouldn't have to return there to the house. I left and filed for a divorce the following week. I was really scared for my life not knowing what would happen next. Things turned out better than I had thought it would, with the help of God.

With the help of God, I made it to my mother's house where I lived for a while until I got things together to move into my own place. With God and my mother's help I was safe once more. For a while but I was still in wonder of who is the person that meant me harm could it have been Bruce? I didn't give him a chance to do what he had planned. Ms. Amonte told me many years ago that this would happen. So I was very careful about who I would let into my inner circle. Bruce was and is out of my life for a while because of my son. Like I said earlier he was super good to my son which made it all the more difficult for me to put a handle on things that were happening. But in the end Bruce became ill at age 55 like he had been told or told me that the Spirit had told him when he was a teenager. And that the Spirit has said and told him that he would only live until he was 56 years old. Bruce passed away after he came to visit my son. I wonder to myself sometimes "how could a person that's so good with children turn out to be so wrong with other people? Bruce died at age 56. Thanks to God and the Holy Spirit I now have no regrets about the past. And I am just glad that it is all over, after all these years. Thank you God!!!, things in my life have been more like normal now.

Chapter 12

"A Night to Remember With Rev. Dye"

Some years ago I went to Birmingham, Alabama as a request by my mother. This was to help out her youngest brother and his wife, who had had a bad stroke. He himself was also in bad health as he had heart problems and was in stage 4 cancer. I didn't really like the idea of moving there, but I told my mother that I would do what I could for a year. I will give them a year to get things together for my aunt to get better if I could. I had not been back to Alabama since I was a baby which is where I was born. That's where me and my two other siblings were born. My mother left with us when I was just a year old. It was very depressing my arrival in Alabama, but I had given my mother my word. First thing I thought was that I couldn't stay there that long. My uncle wasn't forthcoming with anything that he said or did. A lot of lies were told about what he would do. Like compensating me for my duties for him and my aunt, I just let it go, saying to myself that that's the way thing work out sometime. I had other relatives there in the City of Birmingham. But he wouldn't tell me where they were or take me around and introduce me to them. He didn't want me going to the church or anywhere to tell the truth. I think I went to the store twice and he had to take me. No place but the hospital, it was very boring to say the least. During all of this I remember something that Ms. Amonte had told me about this older couple that would not be honest with me and treat me right. Is that it would not be a good fit for me to be with them, and that I wouldn't be treated well. I thought about that over and over but again I was on a mission to help. And God will look kindly on that and bless me.

It turned out to be quite unbearable and quite an ordeal. I really had to pay special attention to what I had to say to my uncle, or he would go off on some kind of tantrum. Or say things like "you know what you can do he would say don't you? Like what now what had I done by listening and believing that things would be okay? As time went by things just became worse. All his lies told me that he had no intentions of carrying out his promises of paying me for my services or anything else. I started looking for a place to stay. I called a couple relatives but they didn't want to help me, they said they didn't know of any places so my mind settled on the house next door to my uncle. I made arrangements by calling the city and asking who owned the house and he was so nice he began work on fixing it up for me. Things were looking up for me right then. It was as if God wanted me to get out of my uncle's house and start over again. I still didn't like the idea of staying in Alabama, but at least now I can go to church again.

I looked around and looked around for a Spiritual church. Then one day I was looking through the phone book I spotted one in walking distance from where the house was. I had moved into the cottage which was a little house when my son arrived in Alabama. I got him to take me around, looking for the church but we couldn't find it as the Ensley area was very hilly and the streets ran every which way. It seemed, especially at night that a person couldn't make out much in the way of traffic and streets. We eventually found it nestled in the hill side. We would have never found it at night. The Church of Life was small. Had about 55 members, it met Sundays' and Wednesdays nights. I really enjoyed the church and the people were giving and helpful for the most part. The Minister was Ella Weast, a Prophet in his own right. A good man, religious, he was out of Boston, New York. The first lady of the church was a person with a calming attitude and very knowledgeable. We got along quite well. The pastors advanced me to the podium or alter whichever you would like to call it. On Wednesday nights I would have time to prophesy to the congregation. It was a wonderful feeling. I saw a lot of miracles occur in the church and other churches also. The pastor would travel to different churches during the week and weekends. We traveled the back roads many evenings and on some Sundays. We would see people with miracles gifts of the Spirit perform unimaginable healing and prophecy to the multitudes of people that would come to hear and see it all in person. People would travel from state to state to get a reading from these magnificent people of God. The name they call this area of the country is the Bible Belt of the South, now I know why.

One evening in the fall of the year we had a special guest to visit the Church of Life. I, myself had never heard of her before that night. The visitor's name was Reverend Mother Dye. She was well built an Afro-American and from what I understand and was told she the Reverend Mother was well known throughout the South in the Bible belt. When Reverend Dye came in she wasn't alone she was with a large group of people that were called her Spiritual band of supporters. It was really something to see that she had that kind of support or influence over a body of followers like that. It was very exciting to see all this in such a small unknown area. The small church was full of people waiting to see her to hear what she had to say and what she would do that evening. The congregation started out with a prayer and the band group performed. They did an opening prayer before the pastor announced Reverend Mother Dye. She prayed for the people of the church and then proceeded into her prophecy healing and the prophecy word for each person call forth. I couldn't believe my ears nor my eyes as I saw the people fall after being prophesied for. She didn't even have to touch them. Some of them I knew myself. I knew they weren't faking because they would fall out with just the wave of her hand in the person's face. And the thing she said was so uncanny. Most of it was so exciting to me; I had never felt that kind of power before. In all the excitement and with everything that was going on I heard a woman voice say Miss please come up here to the podium? I got up out of my chair and went up front. Just as soon as I approached the woman I saw her put something on her hands and rub her hands together. At that very moment she touched my forehead. I immediately went down to the floor. I felt as if I was glued to the floor all I could do was move my eyes, not my head, just my eyes nothing about my body would move. it was as if I was floating downward. I never forgot that feeling as I laid there on the floor, on my back. I tried to move but I couldn't move my head or any part of my body. I could move my eyes from side to side but nothing else. I thought to myself "what just happened to me? It was beautiful the feeling that happened to me as I laid there. I felt the soothing warmth movement of a vibration of some sort move, from the bottom of my feet slowly flowing upward to my thighs to my abdomen and onward over my breast, my entire body to my head to the top of my head. It was beautiful and it felt so good it was warm, it was soothing. I saw someone pick my glasses up and put them on my chest. I tried to move again. Then I said to myself, this is so nice I wish that it would last forever so I just laid there until the feeling faded away. I've seen many miracles but that, I really want to happen again.

Like I said before, I have seen many, many miracles in my lifetime and my having had the gifts since I was a young child. Even so at times it seems so unreal. I have wondered from time to time "how do these gifts that people have truly come about? For me, myself I believe it is from the Holy Spirit of God. Now that I am older, some things have changed with me in how I interpret messages from the Spirits of God and the Holy Spirit. Now I mostly see and hear and see the words. The Spirit of God shows me pictures of different information. In words and sentence form, I still hear the Spiritual Angels speaking to me from time to time especially when I'm giving a message or reading for a person. I thank God for His many gifts that He has given us in this world.

Chapter 13

"Spirituals Healing Power"

Early in my life I started reading and giving messages to people, family members, friends and some strangers that I barely knew. Many people ask me for advice about things in their life. I'm what is called a spiritualist. I can see conditions with health and family and other things with the help of the Holy Spirit. Some readings happen on the consent of the clients with their say so. It's not an invasion of their privacy or the person's rights or anything of that nature. Sometimes maybe I would be visiting or maybe it's an appointment of such. I begin by praying and discerning the spirits as there are different spirits on the other side of life. People are on the other side as they were on this side. If they were liars, cheaters, gossipers or hateful, or envious of others, maybe even tricksters and the like they, the entities, are the same on the other side. this is why you must discern the spirits by praying and asking God to guide you against them while you do your readings and messages and healings for your clientele.

In these several short stories I will tell you of my experiences. Sessions and Spiritual Mediumship with some of my clients, and how the Spirit of God helped me with the healings, hearing and feeling as I deal with these clients with their permission of course. Some cases are very personal. The situations and conditions are heartfelt, for many of these clients. We'll start with Colleen who is my sister-in-law and has a serious or had a serious condition which was taken care of with the help of Spirit of God.

Colleen

On a visit to my sister-in-law's house one day we were sitting and just talking about different things. I was playing around with my nephew Alex. Colleen was sitting on the couch in front of me. I was talking to her when I noticed a green line running up and down from her neck to her chest. I begin to pray and discern the spirit, that was showing me this. I asked Colleen how she felt and did she have any pain in her throat? She said she has some kind of problem but she was scared to go to the doctor with it to see about it. She said that her father had the same problem with his throat before he died she didn't recall what it was called something in his esophagus. But then I saw the green that the Holy Spirit has showed me. With it being green, I thought that it was some kind of an infection of some kind, and that she needed to have it checked out. At that point the Holy Spirit showed me a bottle being held up in the hands of spirit a bottle of medicine and the Holy Spirit "saying that there is medicine for it now". That "everything would be okay", Colleen took my advice and went to the doctor and found out that it may have turned out to be what her father had died from if she had waited much longer. The situation turned out well for Colleen. It's been 20 or more years since that occurrence happened. Colleen and I thank God for his help and her life and mine every day.

Irma a close friend

After, moving to Orlando, Florida some of my clientele followed me. I had some that I spoke to on the phone and some I saw in person. Irma was a lady that I had met and we had talked for some time about spiritual happenings. I could feel that there were problems with Irma in her health. Spirit kept telling me to ask her about things concerning her health, but I put that off until one day I asked her if she wanted a reading. She responded maybe later. So I didn't say much except to say that "there may be something that you may want to look into about your health". This is what the Holy Spirit has said to me about her on that particular day.

Time went by and I finally saw her as she was leaving the complex. She must have been in pain or something because she said okay that she had some time that day to talk with me. We went to my place and I gave her paper and a pen to write down what I was to telling her. We prayed and again I begin to prophesy. I finished the reading and asked her, "if I could put my hands on her stomach" as Spirit had directed me to do. I laid hands on her stomach and the Holy Spirit directed me to tell her that she had an infection throughout her body. I didn't get what kind of infection nor where it was but I told her what Spirit had told me and that she should see a doctor as soon as possible and as soon as you can. I finished as I could see she was very distant in her expression to me. She looked bewildered. She thanked me and left saying that she would like to talk to me sometime later. Which I thought would be in a week or two but I didn't hear from her until I call to check on her, which was some weeks later, when I called. Her daughter answered the phone. I asked to speak to her mother to Irma. Her daughter told me that she wasn't there and that she was in the hospital and had been there for a couple of weeks. Irma's daughter said that Irma had at that time an infection in her body and that the doctor said it ran the gambit through her whole body. The doctors didn't know what it was from at the time we talked.

Irma's daughter and I prayed and ask God for healing and guidance for the situation. Irma eventually was healed by the grace of God and His Angels. Erma later told me that she probably wouldn't have gone to the hospital at the time that she had if I had not told her that the Holy Spirit was telling me that she needed medical help for what was already happening with her. I told Irma that the spirit of God comes to us in our time of need and if we listen to the spirit of God we can avoid much of the pain and the bad things that happened to us in this life thank you God.

Sara's healing

Although, living in Alabama was not my first or best choice of a place to be at that time of my life. I really did enjoy the church life. There I felt free to do what God had put me here to do, and I was given the opportunity to do just that. The people in the two churches I attended seem to know what my purpose was and why I was there with them. It was very inviting and welcoming. We, the congregation traveled a lot and had many festival days at the churches as people gathered to enjoy the times. The people seem to be very engaging with each other. It was more like a huge family affair when they came together to worship.

Sundays we would have worship services and a guest most often at social time afterwards. On Wednesday evenings we would have the same worship, but this would be the time for even more spiritual involvement. At this time the congregation had given me the time to do my thing as a Prophet to the people of the church. This I truly love to do to help guide and hear from the Holy Spirit of God in His Angels. To start my session the band would play that all-encompassing music for the rising of the spiritual vibration. This would change whatever move you were in at that time. Maybe it would be a negative mood it would change that too. This type of spiritual music is hypnotic it has you hanging by a thread forgetting negative cares and putting you in the mood for God to minister to you. After music we were all ready to start the prayer and the prophesying to the people of the church.

On this Wednesday evening, after going through several messages, Spirit told me to call on a lady named Sarah to come up to the podium to be prophesied for. I called on Sarah whom I had seen in the church before, but didn't really know her. Sarah had to have some help coming up to the front of the podium. The men of the church brought her up and they stood behind her in front of me. Then the men stood behind her to break her fall if she was to faint or lose her balance. Sarah had had a stroke and her leg and one of her arms was paralyzed from the stroke. As I stood in front of Sarah at the podium, I heard the voice of the Holy Spirit tell me to tell Sarah that she would be able to use her leg and her arm again. Sarah fell out and the men standing behind her caught her and returned her to her seat. One week later. To my amazement, I saw Sarah in church and she was walking and using her arm. Thank you God we all prayed and worship the Lord my God. The last I heard Sarah was doing well and able to get around and do some of the things she had lost when her arm and leg was disabled. We thank God for these blessings and these healings and we give him all our prayers and Glory.

Mary's Back

While living in California, I had the opportunity to meet up with some very nice people living at the same apartment complex that I lived in. We did lots of things together individually and as groups. It was a very nice complex in the desert of San Bernardino, Ca. There were plenty of mountains and right across the way from the Mountain Resort was Big Bear. There was snow in the mountains, and at Big Bear. And it was very hot around where I live down in the desert. It was a beautiful area. Many days we would meet in the social room of the apartment complex. Just talking or having meetings, just socializing. Mary, Joanne, Shirley, James and many others would be there. Most of the people knew what I did as far as being a Spiritualist. We all went to same church just down and around the corner from the complex. I had been paying attention to Mary for some time. She had a bad a real bad walk and her upper torso was bent over to her waist just about. Mary walked with a cane. I wondered every time I saw her how she could walk it's as bent over as she was. It must have been very painful for her.

One afternoon as we all were having social hour I asked Mary what had happened to make her bent over that way? She said it just happened over time. Before she realized it she was bent all the way over and down. She went to doctors but they didn't help. So she believed that she would be deformed like this for the rest of her life. I have been dealing with Spirit thinking about Mary for some time. Spirit told me that I could help her, but I didn't understand how. I had never seen anyone bent over that way in my life. This day I asked Mary if we could pray together for her condition. Mary said "yes" I had talked to Mary about prophecy before but had never considered lying on of hands on her back for a healing at that time. I continue with the prayers and proceeded to ask Mary to stand up in front of me. At this point I place my one hand on Mary's back and the other hand on her stomach. I massage Mary's back up and down as I move my hands on her back. I asked Mary to stand up straight as she lifted her upper torso. I could hear the bones popping crack and Mary was standing up straight. I asked Mary to bend down again and then up again. I became quite alarmed when I heard the cracks and the pops" oh God "what have I done now? and I said thank you God, Mary and I said it together me and Mary at the same time. Mary was free of whatever it was that had her fixed in that position all these years. Today even though I've moved back to Orlando I still speak to Mary to see how she is doing. She told me that she was doing fine and she does use her cane but she is still upright. I believe that everything happens for a reason and maybe it was Mary's time for a miracle, from God. I truly believe that it was Mary's faith in life. Believe in the Holy Spirit and we will see miracles above miracles to be performed in this lifetime. These people and others have mentioned how their experiences have enriched their lives and have brought them closer to God and the Holy Spirit.

Chapter 14

"God gave me a Way Out"

I was called by my mother to see if I could see my way to help out my aunt and uncle, my mother's youngest brother and his wife in Alabama. I had finished the work on my first book and had some time on my hands. So I figured I could do this thing and do a good deed for someone in need. I decided to do this at the request of my mother. Who seemed very worried at the time for her brother and his wife. My uncle's wife had had a bad stroke and he had heart surgery also. So they were both in pretty bad health. My mother said that they needed some care for about a year until they were able to get some things sorted out about my aunt's care. After talking to my mother and she telling me what the plans were that my uncle had, and was willing to provide for a helper at the time. I decided to give them a year or so until my aunt began to feel better.

I wasn't fond of staying in Alabama, but I decided to do what I could. Despite it having been prophesied that the older couple my aunt and uncle would not be people of their word. That it would turn out to be a bad decision on my part. I felt that I should at least try to help the couple as my mother was so worried about them. So it began to be a mission for me to help my mother with the situation. I put all my effort into preparing myself for this journey as I had promised my mother. So I packed up and moved to Alabama I thought that I knew this Uncle quite well, but to my surprise I didn't know him at all as I thought I did. As time went by I had moved in and taken on caring for the couple. Things were so bad that I decided that I couldn't live with them any longer. I decided to look into the little house next door to them. The house next door was vacant and needed some work. I called the owner through the city assessor's office and explained my situation to him and he agreed to fix the place up for me to live in. He just charged me what I could afford which was a God's blessing as I didn't have much because I wasn't paid for my services by my uncle and Aunt. I was so very thankful; this was a blessing that came just at the right time. It was as if God was still looking over me, despite my nieveness and not heeding the prophecy warnings that were given to me some years earlier by Ms. Amonte.

The highlight of my living in Alabama was the church experiences that I had while I was there. It was beautiful and exciting something I had never experienced before. I wanted to move so badly that there wasn't any money to do that at the time. My mother had become quite ill and I was very worried about her. I got the word from my sister that my mother was having heart failure and was in the hospital. Some of my bills were behind as I had gotten myself into a jam being with my aunt and uncle. Not being paid as was promised my insurance on the house was behind and not being paid I took the payment and got a Greyhound ticket to Grand Rapids, Michigan, to see about my mother as she wasn't doing well at all. I stayed for months and just took care of my mother. That was all that concerned me at the time. I went back and forth to Alabama to take care of business.

I have been at my mother's for about 3 months when my son called me and sent me a picture of a tree that was huge and had fallen on my house. It had torn off the back of the house and the kitchen. Wires were down and all my food was spoiled, he told me. I was sitting in the backseat of my sister's car and she and my mother were sitting in the front seat at the time. When I got the pictures I started to pray because my insurance had lapsed. I didn't have any at the time I figured nothing had happened up to that point and I had it for years. So I figured I could get by until the money came in for me to pay for some more insurance. I didn't have any at the time, I felt lost and abandoned. I didn't know what to do, no place to stay, out of money. "What am I going to do now? And I am in Grand Rapids, Michigan. As I set there almost in tears and fully in shock, I just couldn't believe what my son had just sent me on my phone. I prayed out loud saying what do I do now God? I have nothing. What do I do? At that very moment I heard a Spiritual voice saying "call now and get more new insurance". Don't say anything about the storm and tree falling on the house yet", till Monday". This was Thursday afternoon. This is exactly what Spirit told me to do, and I did it paid down on the new insurance, right there on my phone in the car I did that. I got the insurance; they said it would go into effect by this time the next day. In the meantime I called a spiritual friend advisor that I had known for many years, I was just that nervous. I asked her what was going to happen with the insurance for the storm and house. She told me that she sees two women sitting and discussing my policy one is a supervisor the other is an agent for the insurance company. My spiritual friend said that they would decide to put it through for me which would be a blessing. That Wednesday morning my spiritual advisor told me a Lady by the name of Jessica would call me to tell me what to do. I thanked Terry and waited nervously for that day to arrive. As things happen when you're dealing with a true spiritualist, events will happen as they are supposed to. God has control over all these miracles. As it happened the events turned out just like Terry told me and I received the insurance payment.

With this money I was able to move to California. Which, another prophecy began, and a different life story. With the help of the Holy Spirit I was able to put a very sad and unhappy situation behind me. Which if I had taken into account the prophecies that were given to me at the time; I would have been a lot better off. The words helped me in so many ways, and I can't say enough about it all. The words helped me through so many trying times. That could have been much worse than they were at the time. But with God's help and His Angles I was able to make it out of the terrible situations that I was in. And I am truly thankful for that and will be for the rest of my life, thank you God.

Chapter 15

"Lena Amonte, Spiritualist"

As this is my last book on Living in The Spirit of God by Larna Woods, I want to tell you some things about the woman that influenced me so very much in my life. She gave me hope where there was none at the times that I needed it most.

Ms. Amonte had long black hair and wore it straight back, it came down to her waist. She was pleasantly spoken with a soft voice. It was hard to understand how she would know just when I would call her and ask if I could visit for the day. It seems as if she knew my every thought and moods and what it meant for me to be in her presence at that particular time of the day, which ever time it would be.

It all started, when my brother Jimmy drowned. I was 17 at the time it occurred. I was trying to figure out what to do with my life. I had a small job selling credit cards for Montgomery Wards, but it didn't pay much at all in those days. I had just started out working. I didn't really like the people there they picked and talked about everyone and everything. It was very uncomfortable so I really wanted to find something else. This was the job I was doing when little Jimmy died. I will never forget it. It was a beautiful day, but there was something else about the day. It was different from any other day that I could remember. It was as if I was expecting something to happen that day unusual. I didn't know what to expect not good or bad to be exact but just expecting something that I didn't necessarily want to happen at that time. The dreams about my brother drowning didn't help any at all, but I tried to push them out of my mind. Time and time again my thoughts were settled on them like I had no choice of what I was thinking about.

After the tragedy with my brother Jimmy, someone told my mother about Ms. Amonte. It was told that maybe my mother could get some form of help and understanding with what had happened to her child. My mother started going to see Ms. Amante. It seemed to have a great deal of help and understanding for her at that time. It seemed that my mother began to act more like herself and began to talk more about what had happened to her child with understanding. Mother would often say that she could not understand why God would take her child. Thinking back, it seemed if he was the best one of the bunch at time of his death. He was so thoughtful and obedient, not like the other kids at all.

As I think back to the first time I saw Ms. Amonte

it was somewhat unnerving because every time mother would go see her, mother would come tell me what was said about me. "Why was this I thought, I would think. She ,Ms Amonte , didn't know me but yet would constantly tell my mother everything I was doing. It was my mother who was getting the reading not me. But each time she would tell my mother things about me. I would deny everything maybe not all, but that I that, that I didn't want my mother to know about my life. The guy that I was with at the time, he wasn't much and I didn't know it at the time but it turned out to be a disaster. I wasted many years in that relationship. If I had just listened to Ms. Amonte, I would have had a better life I'm sure of it. But what can you tell the young, most of us don't listen anyway.

Ms. Amonte and I spent many hours talking about God and God's wonders. She studied the stars and planets and told me what relationship they had in our lives. Once she told me that I had to go downtown to the courthouse on some business that I knew about and that I had to do it before the moon changed not one day later or the whole situation would change for me, and I would have to continue to go downtown for a whole year and a half on the situation. Because I did not follow the advice, well it happened, just like I waited a day later before I made up my mind to pursue the case and it took me over a year and a half to get out of it to get out of the Court. When I was young, I didn't listen to well. I have learned better over the years since I've gone through such turmoil since then. As time went by Ms. Amante helped me with many concerns. We talked about everything and she told me about the men in my life about my child, and some friends. Also, there would be situations that would be very difficult for me to handle and much more. It was a good thing knowing her because if she had not been there for me at that time in my life, I fear that I would probably not be here now. As it was that some of the incidents that I have lived through I have been able to avoid them partially because she warned me of that pending occurrence. I had been able to see some of these incidents coming when I would question why or remember what she said to me for that time in my life.

Like for instance, when I was in Alabama and I was feeling and being misused by my aunt and uncle. I was sitting in the chair when I heard her voice describing the room and the lamp that was behind the couch that she had told me about, and she said that when I remembered that I would know that things would get better and she said that I would make it out of that situation, and have my own place. That was such a relief for me because my money didn't go far as they had decided that they were not going to pay me as they had promised. The money came to and I was able to move out of Alabama, which was another one of God miracles. As to how it happened in my time of need. I learned so much from her about how the stars and planets line up with other planets and the moon, Mars and, Jupiter, Which helps and tells us how and when to do certain things to come. When will the best time be to make a certain move decision or position a move or just stop stay put for a time or do it all at once. When I did listen to her directions things would turn out favorable in my behalf. Which I found out to listen and have things turn out better than worse. I learned this by trial and error. I knew quite a few people that went to her from time to time, but they said that they never had much time to spend with her. It would be in and out for them. Get their reading and be gone. I didn't understand that because whenever I would call her she would just say "I'm waiting for you honey". Then I would go and spend the day with her. No one would come over or bother us for that time that we spent together. It was beautiful we spent time in her garden. She told me about her life and some of the people that were in her life. Ms. Amonte 's husband had died sometime before leaving her with two teenage daughters. This is when she decided to come to America. She worked and raised her daughters. Ms. Amonte was a native of Italy. I remember seeing her daughters. One was very beautiful I imagine Ms. Amonte being like her in her youthfulness. The one thing Ms. Amonte would say is that the oldest daughter would be her punishment. Spending and doing too much for the beautiful one. She was her heart and joy and that would be her punishment from God before she passed over to the other side. The other was a red headed very plump with freckles. Not as beautiful just on the heavy side with a nice disposition. This Ms. Amonte said that she had not spent time and money and affection on this one as much as she did the other, and this would be a burden that she would have to bear for the rest of her life.

God showed her a vision of what her life was going to be like. It will be like the red-headed child would come to her and rescue her when the beautiful black hair daughter that had broken her and taken all that she had left in life. Ms. Amonte told me about her vision and said that there was nothing that would or could change the will of God. I listened and life continued on for us both of us. I thought about what she said often and wished that it would not happen that way for her.

As the years went by, I continue to live through what the prophecy had for my future. Some good some bad, I moved back to Grand Rapids, Michigan after living in Detroit for about 9 years. I thought about Ms. Amonte, as my mother and I sat at the table one morning my mother said that she hadn't heard anything about her in years. I was anxious to see and talk to her again, such a long time had gone by. My mother and I set out calling and asking people if they had seen or heard anything about her. No such luck in responses. Until one day my mother had to go downtown to the courthouse to take care of some business. To my mother's surprise we found out something about her.. My mother walked out of the courthouse right in front of her, Ms. Amonte. Mother said they talked a while and exchanged phone numbers. My mother said Ms. Amonte was pleading for her independence to stay her own guardian and to care for herself. Her oldest beautiful daughter wanted her possessions that she had brought with her over from the old country, her dolls and such things worth a great deal of money. We stayed in touch, and she was living with her red-headed daughter at that time. Rose had rescued her mother from her sister. I went to see Ms. Amonte a few years later and it was as she had told me she would be, as a big rag doll, no control over her body but she would still have her mind and know me. I went to Rose house to see Ms. Amante. That's where she was living at the time. Rose told me that she didn't think her mom could even remember me or anyone at that time in her life. Rose said we'll see I said "okay" Rose led me to the bedroom where Ms. Amonte was lying in the bed. Rose said Mom there is someone here to see you. Ms. Amante just laid there, then Rose lifted her up by her torso and Rose sat down on the bed by her Rose lifted Ms. Amonte's head and placed it on her shoulder and then pull her legs out of the bed. I was so shocked it was just liked she had said it would be. She was like a big rag doll. Rose asked her mother "do you know who this is? Ms. Amonte said "yes" I used to get you and your mother mixed up". I thought to myself that the vision had come true for Ms. Amonte. She was in body but a big rag doll, but just like God had told her in the vision she would have her mind until the end. She remembered me and I am still living through the words that God gave her for me.

Conclusion

The overall knowledge that I want to express in this book, "Living in The Spirit of God", is a feeling of hope and fulfillment and knowing that there is always a superior entity out there in the universe and around us always that protects, guilds', and nourishes us through this life. Many of us don't know about these spiritual happenings or miracles as I will call them. They are all around us and many of us possess the gifts of the Holy Spirit and don't know that yet. As I have walked through life ups and downs I have become a witness for God and His Angels workings. The Holy Spirit is all around us every minute and second of the day and night. I hope and pray that the short but true stories make an impression on you.

You may go through some difficult times in your own life look inside yourself for the power you need to go on with this life, remember I had a lot of help because I didn't understand and was ignorant to the facts of life. For the most part I did not listen. I know better now, by listening to life's challenges and heeding the warning signs we can learn a lot. We can learn how to avoid a lot of the grief that sometimes catches up with us when we're off guard. For this I give knowledge, thanks and love to God and the Holy Spirit.